What Just Happened

Harnessing Wellness Ideas for trying to cope with the "New Normal" following the COVID-19 pandemic

Naomi Rossthorn

Copyright © 2023 Naomi Rossthorn

ISBN: 978-1-922954-55-8

All rights reserved. This book may not be reproduced or used in any manner whatsoever without the express written permission of the publisher except for the use of brief quotations in a book review.

For express permission for reproducing materials please contact:

Naomi Rossthorn
www.harnessingwellness.com

Disclaimer

This book is not a replacement for any type of traditional therapy, counselling, cognitive behavioural therapy or medicated interventions. This book is an overview of key topics related to mental health and wellbeing, and hopefully a way for people to read, debrief and normalise for themselves and others *what just happened?*

DEDICATION

This book is dedicated to:
Everyone who was impacted by Covid-19.
My family, who support me, for which I am grateful.
My clients, to whom I am indebted. Thank you for trusting me.
The key workers – thank you for your service during and after the pandemic.

CONTENTS

Introduction	i
1. Holistic Therapy	1
2. Mental Health Pre-Pandemic	19
3. Agoraphobia and Social Anxiety	29
4. The Impact of School Closures on Wellbeing	35
5. The Societal Divide	41
6 . Lockdown Fatigue	45
7 . Collective Social Anger	49
8. The Power of Fear	53
9. The Impact of Unemployment	57
10. Work, Overworking, and Key Workers	61
11. Bereavement and Loss	67
12. Existential Change and Metamorphosis	73
Conclusion	77
About the Author	79
References	81

INTRODUCTION

On Tuesday 11 January 2022 my family contracted COVID-19. We had been through many lockdowns here in Melbourne Australia and were out of lockdown at the time. As a family, we had been conservative about the places we had gone and are still not sure how my oldest son contracted COVID.

He was complaining of being too tired to brush his teeth – he was eleven years old, so we thought he was just tired and trying to get out of it. He was laying down in the hallway opposite the bathroom. This behaviour was a bit extreme for him, so I tested him for COVID-19.

I cried when the two red lines appeared. I was frightened, as I had heard stories about the worst-case scenarios due to my work as a psychologist. After my 11-year-old, myself and my youngest son, 6 years old and asthmatic, contracted the virus. Then finally my husband tested positive.

I had never been so unwell – it felt like my nervous system was burning. I called my mother, a retired nurse, at 3am crying, asking her what to do. I was scared I was dying. My mother – a matron type – told me take some Panadeine, try to sleep and call her at first light. The next day was a little bit better. I have since lived with long COVID symptoms, and it has taken a year for them to subside.

My husband and I were both vaccinated; however, my children weren't – they had been scheduled to be vaccinated on the Friday. Family and neighbours brought us food; the experience showed us the real value of community and friendship. We were fearful about touching or passing it on to others. It brought about many emotions – fear, anxiety, relief – as well as the sickness itself.

I wrote this book using 'talk to text' initially, before, during and after my experience of getting COVID. Having worked as a psychologist, I had worked with people experiencing the same difficulties – fear, vulnerability, isolation, stress, juggling home-schooling and work, children's fears, and social isolation – that I was experiencing myself. For the first time, there was a blurring of boundaries, which meant it was harder to hold a balanced psychological space in which to work with clients. There was no reprieve from work to home to work.

This book overviews my thoughts with some research to support key areas of the issues as they are written.

So, if you are currently reading this book; it means you have survived the pandemic, which would have entailed more than just physically avoiding all that the disease can cause; it's not just physical survival, but mental, emotional, and social survival.

In Australia we started hearing about a respiratory virus at the end of December 2019. There were reports of an infection originating from a single city in China that spread around the entire country. Officials were greatly concerned by the seriousness of the illness and its rapid spread.

INTRODUCTION

COVID-19 battled its way through countries and populations, and, at the time of writing, has caused 275 million cases of illness and 5.3 million deaths according to the World Health Organisation. Some survivors have struggled to recover their previous physical health, suffering from long-term disabling symptoms such as breathlessness, fatigue, heart palpitations, and tinnitus. The condition is known as long COVID.

The COVID-19 pandemic is one of the most disruptive forces that we have experienced in humankind for millennia. It has caused a devastating amount of loss, destruction, grief, and financial ruin. Predominantly social beings, humans were forced into periods of isolation that went against every instinct of our nature. Restrictions of varying severities were imposed in nearly every single country, with very few people escaping any mental detriment.

Schools were closed.

Offices and workplaces were vacated.

People's homes became their offices.

The roads became deserted, with few cars rolling through.

Supermarkets were filled with mass hysteria.

No toilet paper was left on the shelves.

Sanitiser was everywhere.

Face masks were produced en masse.

And as chaos spread, we waited indoors and watched our world crumble before us on the news.

COVID-19 demonstrated vulnerabilities that existed in our already fragile manmade ecosystem. The healthcare system was challenged and sometimes brought it to its knees. Care homes for the elderly or disabled became isolation rooms and subsequently graveyards. Schools were abandoned.

Everyday life seemed to be turned on its head, and what this book will explore is the collective grieving process that people around the world experienced as they regretted not taking that last opportunity to go dancing, to have a barbecue with friends, or hug a loved one.

The impact on mental health worldwide has been immense. While it can't be measured, it must not be forgotten. What is forgotten is in danger of being repeated, and we don't want history to repeat itself. There are lessons to be learned from this experience. This is an ongoing dialogue.

Millions of people around the world woke up to a harsh lesson about their life, their relationships, and the purpose of their existence on Earth. COVID-19 forced people to change their way of life in a rapid fashion; physically and mentally, people had to quickly adapt to a new lifestyle. This caused upset for many people across the world, as the world they knew was completely turned on its head.

To contain the rapid spread of COVID-19, drastic measures such as isolation and quarantine were introduced. People were prevented from human contact; in shops, schools, birthday parties, weddings, funerals – a wide range of everyday occasions and momentous life events, such as the birth of a baby.

Inevitably, as this was a brand-new virus, there was little research on the impact of COVID-19, let alone tips and tricks for how to survive in a pandemic. Pandemics and their impact had very little research, and the study of humans in forced isolation is also small. This makes every piece of research on COVID-19 and how to survive the mental trauma of loneliness and illness very useful.

Acknowledging feelings of distress and isolation is therapeutic, as avoiding the issue can cause complications for years to come. This book aims to help people explore mental, emotional, spiritual and physical wellbeing.

Perhaps the most inspiring message that was spread was the consistent message of hope. Hope within a neighbourhood, hope with family and friendships. Throughout this pandemic, communities pulled together. Mother Nature began to heal herself. Families spent more time together than ever, sometimes this was good sometimes not so good. The benefits of working from home were experienced. For some, debts have been repaid. Others experienced loss of business or change of lifestyle.

This guide will normalise your experience of the pandemic, defining what your 'normal' is and aligning it to the 'new' normal we are experiencing as a collective. It doesn't claim to be therapy, nor is a replacement for a good, qualified therapist. If you are suffering from any mental distress or just don't feel like yourself, you should consider arranging a meeting with your trusted medical practitioner to advise you regarding therapy or counselling sessions.

However, what this book will aim to provide is hope. Hope, and the ability to address your traumatic experiences in writing, acknowledge them, and support you to let them go if they no longer serve you.

So please, read, remember, and reminisce on the lessons that the pandemic gifted us – the good, the bad, and the distressing. Only once we learn can we heal and focus on rebuilding an even better world than we had before. Take care.

1

HOLISTIC THERAPY

You treat a disease, you win, you lose – you treat a person, I guarantee you, you'll win, no matter what the outcome.

Robin Williams as the title role in the movie *Patch Adams* **(1998)**

Holistic is a word that describes the treatment of a whole person – mentally, socially, and emotionally – rather than just treating the symptoms of a disease. Studies have shown that a holistic approach is the best solution to combat COVID-19 and its after-effects, rather than a purely medical approach solely treating physical symptoms (Kotwani et al 2021). In addition, its traditional treatment – solo isolation with no contact except medical professionals – can have severe and profound mental health consequences.

Holistic therapy can include a wide range of treatments, including a varied diet, vitamin consumption, exercise, music therapy, art therapy, outdoor exposure (in a controlled environment) for fresh air and vitamin D, and fun games. This type of treatment considers the whole patient rather than just the symptoms of the medical condition COVID-19; therefore, has a much higher success rate. The patient survives with fewer traumatic memories than those who just had their physical symptoms alleviated.

What Does Holistic Recovery Look Like?

Stress reduction
The COVID-19 pandemic placed a multitude of different stresses on the shoulders of humanity. Stresses from work, due to the threat of being made redundant or furloughed; stresses from the impending, inevitable illness; health concerns through the roof; agoraphobia; social anxiety; the worry of not being able to pay bills. Stress for medical professionals and others trying to avoid contracting the virus and being put in unusual situations to do this.

The stress of wearing masks, personal protective gear, and other strategies to avoid exposure. Reducing the effects of stress, was and is so important to mental and physical health. People in workplaces requested to work outside their position description and complete tasks unknown to them.

These stresses can manifest in physical forms such as migraines, stomach issues, back pain, teeth grinding, and muscle tension. Reducing stress and the effects of stress may be different for everyone, but here are some ideas.

Outdoor activity

Regular outdoor activity boosts the body's levels of vitamin D, supporting a healthy immune system. Time spent in nature is also associated with improving mental wellbeing and lowering stress levels. Being in nature allows our senses to slow down, take in the moment. Nature is slower in movement in comparison to a freeway, for example. We can notice five things we can see, notice five things we smell, notice five things we can touch and really bring our awareness back into the moment. This exercise of noticing five things can be taught to children through to adults. It is an easy one to remember when stressed.

Eating well

Eating healthy, natural foods is vital to our health and wellbeing. Dark leafy greens, bright citrus fruits, powerful energy-boosting carbohydrates, and healthy fats all contribute to our hair, skin, teeth, nails, and immune system, fighting off COVID-19.

Getting into nature

Research your national parks and reserves to explore a nature trail you haven't walked. If you live in a city, look at your local area to find a car journey to your nearest nature reserves. Whether it is a beach, a forest, the bush, or simply the local park, any fresh oxygen out in nature is beneficial for wellbeing. Consider going barefoot – known as 'grounding', research shows that the connection of bare feet to a natural substance such as grass, sand or soil can reduce inflammation, pain and improve sleep (Chevalier et al 2012).

Moving daily

Whether it is running or dancing, walking, stretching or yoga, pilates, weights, commit to a daily dose of exercise and activity each day. Even cooking in your kitchen can be a workout – incorporate regular movement into your everyday activities, such as three minutes of star jumps while you wait for water to boil. Movement is especially supportive of wellbeing for those in isolation due to COVID-19. After having COVID, I no longer had the energy go to the gym and lift weights.

Instead, I started Pilates and have really enjoyed it. Counting steps is another way to make a goal for movement. Research varies on this, but you should aim for 7,000 to 10,000 steps a day. According to the Heart Foundation (10000steps.org.au), walking can:

- increase energy
- improve mood and confidence
- provide a sense of achievement
- help with relaxation
- reduce your risk of heart attack
- help with weight management
- promote healthier blood pressure
- build stronger bones and muscles

Play and leisure

It's not just for children! As adults, including play, rest, and leisure activities in your everyday routine is vital for your health and wellbeing. Find a way of playing that lights you up.

Perhaps it's bowling, dancing, tennis, video games, or a simple card game played with friends. Whatever the outlet, play and leisure are vital for your mental health and wellbeing. There are plenty of play and leisure activities that you can also conduct in isolation, such as yoga, reading and meditation, meaning that self-isolation due to COVID-19 doesn't have to take a serious toll on your mental health and wellbeing.

For motivation, get a few friends or family together online and perhaps do the activities via phone or video. This will encourage a sense of connection, motivation, and group wellbeing.

Mental Health and Wellbeing

Wellbeing, the state of being well, can manifest itself in different ways for different people. This is because wellbeing is all about 'being well in yourself'; but as everybody is an individual, everyone will have a different level of satisfaction with their own selves and lives. Mental health is how people perceive the world and function inside of it; therefore, it is completely subjective to each person.

There are many factors, both internal and external, that influence wellbeing. External factors such as employment, income, living conditions and social circles can either raise or lower your wellbeing. Internal factors such as optimism, self-confidence and resilience can boost wellbeing. When you reflect on these areas of your life and consider how they can be improved, you can see how to actively improve your wellbeing.

Wellbeing can be measured in several different ways, but the most important one is considering how someone really feels about their life. Are they hopeful for the future?

Are they improving themselves or something else in their lives? Are they isolated or lonely? Do they believe their life has meaning? These are only a few, but there are many factors that indicate whether a person's wellbeing is ranked high or low.

Happiness and wellbeing are synonyms, but they have slightly different meanings. The overall focus should be on wellbeing, as wellbeing covers all aspects of your health rather than only an emotional state.

Wellbeing was a challenge to manage during the COVID-19 pandemic; those who were vulnerable to mental health conditions experienced an exacerbation of symptoms such as suicidal ideation, self-harming, eating disorders, depression, a defeatist attitude, and a sense of 'entrapment' (O'Connor et al 2021). People who were significantly more vulnerable to these symptoms included women, people aged 18–29, and those living in socially disadvantaged circumstances.

In the cited study, it was discovered that although loneliness and depression maintained a steady rate throughout all peaks and troughs of the pandemic, suicidal thoughts increased as the pandemic and lockdowns continued. Due to this, governments, health professionals, and other support people across the world took a proactive approach towards wellbeing and mental health.

This is why this book is so important; not as a replacement for therapy, but to provide multiple coping strategies for those who are struggling to make it through each day. You are not alone. I continue to see clients (it is now June 2023) who refer to the impact of the pandemic has had on their mental health, their children's and family and friends.

Holistic Therapy in Addition to Medical Interventions

This book does not contend that medical treatment should be stopped in favour of alternative therapies. In all cases of COVID-19, the physical symptoms should be treated to stop the progression of the disease. However, in most cases, a holistic approach of diet, exercise, mindfulness, connection, and other outlets can assist to support a boost in mental recovery from COVID-19, or even to support a person during or after isolation.

In all cases, it's recommended that when recovering from severe symptoms of COVID-19, the holistic treatment begins with a phased return to work. This is potentially limited by the socioeconomic circumstances of the person; however, government funding options should be explored to make sure the person doesn't return to their previous work pattern too quickly (Chopra et al 2020). Returning to work is important, as returning to work after COVID-19 is associated with an improved quality of life and reduced depression, most likely due to the sense of purpose that a job brings (Peake et al 2021).

Globally, people have tried different things. In the UK, over 2.5 million clinically vulnerable patients were offered free vitamin D supplements to support their bone development, muscle health, and general immune system health. This included residents of care homes and patients in hospitals.

During autumn and winter, it is generally advisable to take extra vitamin D, especially in colder countries such as the United Kingdom. This was especially relevant for patients who isolated over the summer months and therefore didn't get adequate vitamin D levels when the sun was at its strongest. Studies from Harvard Medical School advocate that vitamin C, zinc, vitamin D and melatonin show positive effects on immune boosting functions, however, provide no efficacy on antiviral loads (Hemilä and Chalker 2013; Hemilä 2017).

Therefore, if you are considering supplementation, they should only be used as a complement to modern medicine, not a replacement. Further advice could be sought.

Holistic therapy may be useful for the treatment of long COVID, which is the official diagnosis for patients experiencing symptoms 30 days after testing positive for COVID-19. 'It's not just looking at the pulmonary issues, but really looking at cardiac, neurocognitive and behavioural issues while helping the patient navigate the system,' says Dr. Sousa, pulmonologist, and critical care physician at Atlantic Medical Group.

Holistic support includes peer support groups, so people feel heard and understood. They receive empathy from somebody who truly understands their symptoms and quality of life. Matching patients with other patients with symptoms of the same severity or longevity is valuable for improving a person's sense of community and reducing isolation. I am working with a number of client's who have presented with change in functioning due to long COVID-19 and this has changed their mental health and wellbeing.

Dr Elaine Maxwell, Clinical Adviser at the National Institute for Health Research (NIHR) Dissemination Centre, conducted a meta-analysis of over 300 papers and discovered that there was a need for an urgent re-evaluation of the contemporary care model, suggesting that 'long COVID is a multi-system' disease and therefore needs multi-system, multi-professional care rather than a purely medical management of the symptoms (Maxwell 2020).

How Has COVID-19 Changed Social Structures

Man is by nature a social animal; an individual who is unsocial naturally and not accidentally is either beneath our notice or more than human. Society is something that precedes the individual. Anyone who either cannot lead the common life or is so self-sufficient as not to need to, and therefore does not partake of society, is either a beast or a god.

Aristotle

Humans are inherently social beings. Happier people tend to have deeper, more meaningful family and friendships, which in turn increases their success. When humans are around other humans, it provides a sense of reassurance that we belong to part of a social group. Humans thrive in positive social environments, and we do our best work in a supportive team. This is partly due to our increased sense of belonging, which traces back to our ancestral fear of being 'isolated' from our fellow cavemen.

In those days, to be excluded from the tribe meant certain death. The group meant safety, hence the phrase 'safety in numbers'. Nowadays we have no predators to run from, but being connected does give us a strong, supportive network of peers who can offer advice and support when the going gets tough. This situation is reciprocal – you should always be there for people in a time of crisis.

Belonging to a group of people can improve your self-worth. You become someone's 'friend', a companion, something valuable and precious in someone's life. This vastly improves your mental health and your outlook on life.

However, this becomes a catch-22 – to be happy, you must have strong social connections; however, to have strong social connections, you need to show yourself as a happy-go-lucky character. And when you add lockdowns and a pandemic into the equation, this greatly complicates social structures. Social structures may have been strained in isolation and separation may have added stress to being separated.

Remote Working

Working from home brought people a new sense of satisfaction. No longer did people have to face the daily commute or whole workday stuck in front of their office computer, clock watching. Instead, people were allowed to work from the comfort of their own homes – even in pyjamas if they wanted to!

Apart from flexible workwear, other benefits of working from home included less commuting time, improved flexibility over the working day, reduced staff turnover and less staff sickness due to not being exposed to bacteria, the flu and COVID-19.

Some limitations faced by remote workers include the lack of social interaction, reduced motivation, reduced exercise, and fatigue from lack of structure. The McKinsey Global Institute argues that 'Many of such jobs are low wage and more at risk from broad trends such as automation and digitization. Remote work thus risks accentuating inequalities at a social level' (McKinsey & Company 2020).

In addition, less economically developed countries didn't have the technological infrastructure to work from home, meaning they were more susceptible to exposure to COVID-19.

At the time of writing this, it is looking like a hybrid remote working may be here to stay. In this way, the pandemic highlighted alternative ways of working, and has broken through technological walls, forcing companies to use online platforms inventively.

It has also caused an attitude shift; employers had to develop a sense of trust in their employees, that they would still work even with the distraction of home life around them. Seeing clients via telehealth options allowed continued access to mental health care during the pandemic. This was useful in increasing access to mental health support through lockdowns.

Collective Grief

Around the world, our communities suffered. The losses have stacked against each other, one by one, and they can be felt in every country, across every set of people, in every language. As humans, we are not used to this worldwide sense of collective grief; but it is something we must learn to understand and perhaps live with, accept and move forward from.

We are grieving for our general sense of safety. Previously, some humans thought they were untouchable. Immortal. The pandemic bought to light, in this situation that people were not always in control of their lives – no matter how well you eat, or how much you exercise, there are factors beyond human control that can take life away in the blink of an eye. 'We've lost that sense of certainty, that sense of safety, that sense of predictability and so it stands to reason that all of that leaves us feeling dislocated and unsure about what's going to happen next,' says Phyllis Kosminksy, president of the Association for Death Education and Counselling.

To move on from the feeling of insecurity and uncertainty, it is important to be kind to yourself. Find tiny moments of gratitude and joy in the everyday ache of the loss. Even if it's just a cup of coffee in the morning, it's important to find one thing in the day that you were grateful for.

Something that was familiar can also be reassuring, such as walking in the sunshine and enjoying the feeling of it on your face. Showing gratitude or being thankful or grateful is expressing or experiencing the feeling of appreciation of a moment – the environment, kindness, a gift, support, or help. Practising gratitude each day has been shown to increase mental and physical wellbeing. I am more thankful for not being locked down, for being able to see friends and family and for my children to be able to attend school.

In some situations we are grieving the loss of our social connections, and these may have changed. From only being able to wave at loved ones through windows. From the social rituals that we missed, such as graduations, Christmas, weddings, and funerals. We mourned our daily routine that felt so familiar and so safe.

Liz Ritchie, a psychotherapist from St. Andrew's Healthcare, said 'Whether we realise it or not, the last couple of years is testament to the fact that we are resilient and we can adapt. We've surprised ourselves really, the coping mechanisms we have are very effective, and often we don't even realise we are doing it' (Jackson 2021).

Keep your eyes on the future when disappointment rears its head at yet another cancelled family event. Remind yourself that this too shall pass, and your event will eventually happen when it is safest to do so.

We are grieving the loss of our financial security. Now, more than ever, we can see that jobs and careers are more fragile than we thought. There are more empty shops in our local area, I too had to close one of my offices. Losing money is concurrent with losing your lifestyle; the little luxuries you are used to are no more.

Also, as finances, bills, and debt are typically a 'taboo' subject amongst friends, it is more important than ever to be honest about your monetary woes with those close to you. If that still feels uncomfortable, when the thoughts of money loss are overwhelming, put pen to paper and write it out. Write out the facts, such as your outgoings and upcoming bills, and then write a list of ways you can generate money before those payments come out.

Join money-saving groups online to foster your sense of community, reduce feelings of isolation, and realise that there is a collective of people out there who are experiencing financial anxiety as well.

We are grieving the loss of our security which can be known as 'anticipatory grief', it is the awful feeling of not getting your hopes up because the future is so uncertain. Our brain has registered the dire events of the pandemic and is internally telling us that it could rear its ugly head again, bringing another lockdown.

It is very rare that humankind ever loses its collective sense of safety, possibly not since the last flu pandemic in

1918. If this is you, and you are experiencing anticipatory grief and it's robbing you of your present-day happiness, it's important to do grounding activities to bring you back into the present.

Mindfulness and meditation are easily accessible if you remember to bring yourself back into the room. Name five things you can feel, touch, hear, see – think as basic as possible, from the wind outside to the floor under your feet. Sometimes people prefer movement to being stationary for relaxation. Walking may be more suitable for you.

To manage anticipatory grief, you can also practise dividing issues into events you realistically can control versus events you can't control. Situations and events you realistically can control – such as panicking about visiting a friend who has suddenly developed a cough – you could manage, for example, by rescheduling the day out. Manage it in a way that doesn't bring more stress to your life. For events you can't control, you should acknowledge the feelings of anxiety. Thank your brain for trying to protect you in a primitive way, and let the thoughts go.

Another factor you can improve is the feeling of loneliness brought on by the pandemic; by expanding your friendship circle through the power of the internet. Your emotional wellbeing is influenced by the actions of other people – we know that happiness is contagious, and that a strong social network is the key to long lasting happiness. If you are still in search of your forever friends, isolation has brought on feelings of loneliness, and you worry about returning to the outside world, consider joining online social groups such as a book club, or a fitness support group.

Then, think of the events you can't control. These are events such as government decisions, the spread of the virus, whether people you love get sick or not. Make a physical list of the things you can't control, and what it is about these events happening that makes you feel anxious. Now, decide – are you obsessing over the problems, or are you problem-solving? If the answer is obsession, ruminating, going over the problems again and again, without thinking of a practical solution for them, then this will not solve any problems for you, only create more in your mind. Write down ideas for solving the problem, what alternatives do you have?

The New Normal

'The new normal' is when an unfamiliar or atypical situation becomes standard. It manifests in new patterns of behaviour forced upon you due to an unexpected life event, such as the pandemic. When your life and routine are turned upside down, it's important to continue to meet and recognise your basic human needs, which is why a 'new normal' must be established. However, emotionally it can be distressing to adapt to a new routine – especially if you were satisfied with your old one.

Even more upsetting can be comparing yourself with others on social media. One day, you are berating yourself for not taking your daily walk and taking the time to rest on your sofa, which is a perfectly valid form of self-care. However, when you scroll through social media, you see people have uploaded glossy, edited photos of them jogging on the beach, their muscles ripped, with a healthy tan and a big smile beaming on their face. You can't help but feel the pang of jealousy; why can't I do that?

Be honest with yourself about how you're feeling, and don't be afraid to make use of the tools that social media gives us to handle these feelings of envy. Tools such as 'mute, unfollow, delete, restrict' are all available across the various social media platforms. You are the person responsible for improving your own mental health; and if social media is detrimental to that, consider going cold turkey.

In the new normal, it is vital to find an escape from the everyday drudgery of the pandemic. Finding distractions – ideally not on social media, as above – is important, as are regular breaks from screen time. Use this time to discover a new hobby, learn a new language, or express your feelings through art.

Once you find your new routine, try to stick to it as much as you can for your own mental health. This will help your mind to cope with the adjustments; your body and brain thrive on routine, so waking up at the same time and going to bed at the same time every day is a basic building block to improving your mental health.

Also, escape the news cycle – the news can be addictive in a crisis, especially as updates are happening hour by hour. Tell yourself, 'If it's important, I'll hear about it somehow', and switch off the news. Or give yourself one hour of allotted news time – ideally in the evening, so the news can't ruin the start of your day. Fill your day with good news – there are dedicated good news channels and media feeds, which remind you of all the good happening in the world.

Setting boundaries is vital for your emotional wellbeing, however many people find setting boundaries difficult, especially with loved ones. Setting boundaries comes from understanding where you are in the process – are you in survival mode, just trying to get through each day? Are you in thrive mode, where you have successfully mastered your new routine, and found ways to make your new normal even better than your previous life? Respect where you are at and give yourself self-compassion if you are not where you want to be just yet. Find ways of discussing sensitively where your family and friends are at. If they are at the opposite ends to you, set some emotional and energetic boundaries.

Once you understand each other's wants and needs and can communicate this in a respectful manner, it really reduces the capacity for friction and tension. Setting boundaries in a pandemic and afterwards can sound like many different phrases. For example:

'Would you be willing to self-isolate before we meet, to be on the safe side?'

'Would everyone mind getting tested beforehand, and only coming if negative?'

2

MENTAL HEALTH PRE-PANDEMIC

Every transformation demands as its precondition 'the ending of a world' – the collapse of an old philosophy of Life.

Carl Jung

Before the 2020 global pandemic, there were indicators that mental health issues were increasing and already on the verge of disrupting our health services. Mental health services were already strained by cuts to government funding, making the sufferers extremely vulnerable.

Having pre-existing mental health conditions before the pandemic predisposes you to a higher level of depression and anxiety during lockdowns.

Research from the University College of London confirmed this, co-led by Professor Nishi Chaturvedi who said: 'The anxiety and depression experienced by the participants of the study go beyond the mental ill health reported to GPs and healthcare services. This is a largely hidden group of people vulnerable to potentially long-lasting health and socioeconomic consequences of the pandemic' (Open Access News 2021).

To avoid vital services being overstretched even more, it is important to make sure that healthcare and mental health support is easily accessible for those who need it the most. This includes medication access, access to procedures, clinics, and appointments, and being able to access income and housing.

Absence of these leads to economic downfall from being too mentally unwell to attend work, or even being furloughed or made redundant by their employer. This means even more stress and duress on a person who is already clinically vulnerable to mental health conditions. It is vital to be able to identify the people in your life who are clinically vulnerable and predisposed to mental health issues, making sure you reach out to them and offer support or assistance finding support they need.

Groups At Risk

One group at risk of mental health issues is people living alone. Millions of people have felt lonely during the pandemic, but if you live by yourself, this is especially exacerbated.

People who lived in share house or other arrangements where those present were not close friends may have also felt lonely and isolated from loved ones.

Thanks to modern technology, being isolated and still communicating with others is much easier than during the 1918 flu pandemic. You can phone or videocall a friend or family member – even a qualified therapist is now just a call away.

If you know you have elderly neighbours who are at risk of being alone, conduct a doorstep visit as safely as possible. If restrictions permitted, regular visits to share something with them, such as cooking or baked goods. COVID-19 showed us just how important a good neighbourly spirit is, especially for the elderly and alone.

Being a key worker such as a nurse or care worker and being regularly exposed to the virus is likely to cause detrimental health consequences. Studies by the British Medical Journal concluded that key workers were at higher risk of catching the virus, therefore suffered from low moods, higher anxiety, and increased stress levels. There were medical staff presenting for psychological counselling having panic attacks on the way to work, unable to enter hospitals and nursing homes.

Furthermore, due to their frequent exposure to the virus, they were more likely to be isolated from their non-key worker family and friends. If this is relatable to you as a key worker, it's important to seek support or talk to your line manager about how you are feeling, as they may be able to implement effective advice and support to help you through a difficult period at work.

Most Common Mental Health Issues

Stress
The physical symptoms of stress include a variety of psychological and physical symptoms such as racing heart, internal anger, lashing out irrationally, changed eating habits (e.g. bingeing/restriction), and partaking of addictive

behaviours such as smoking, drinking or gambling. Sound like you? It sounds like stress could be seeping into your life.

Rigorously plan your working hours, particularly if you are working from home and boundaries are often crossed. Have a strict time where you will stop working and stick to it by rewarding yourself for following your routine. Keep a static diary and plan your weekly activities adding time for self-care and family. Sticking to it may be hard; however, 'training' ourselves to follow a structure may be helpful and allow better self-care.

Anxiety

Anxiety can manifest itself through difficulty sleeping; increase in substance use such as alcohol, smoking, and drugs; and deteriorating physical health due to the emotional toll anxiety plays on the immune system.

Children who look up to their parents and caregivers for emotional support and guidance became more anxious and scared of catching COVID during the pandemic and even now. Children at schools are refusing to go when there are others unwell in their class. Talking through how to keep safe by washing hands and other infection control procedures can give your children some ideas for 'staying safe'.

Keeping an open dialogue and reducing access to social media and the news may also support children manage anxiety regarding COVID-19.

Young people are also affected by anxiety – this was aggravated by the closure of universities, places of education, changes in routine, reduced face to face social interaction with peers and loss of income during the pandemic. If you are in this category, carefully filter what information you receive on social media – fake news is everywhere, and you don't want to see something that makes you feel worse.

We are yet to see the long term emotional, social, and developmental impacts of lockdowns on babies, children, and adolescents. I know my children can be more anxious around social settings and catching sickness.

Pandemic Flux Syndrome

Do you remember the little rituals we had before the pandemic? We would all take a birthday cake and blow all over it, sharing germs and not tidying up. We would share a bowl of nuts and crisps with complete strangers at the bar, dipping our grubby fingers in and out.

Pandemic flux syndrome refers to the whiplash effect of opening up after lockdown. For example, when you return to something after it has been closed and you feel over the moon, but you are emotionally not ready for the changes the pandemic will bring.

With the pandemic, humans are constantly changing between healthy and sick, coming and going, home working and office, online and offline. Flitting between these two states is known as 'pandemic flux'.

Mental Health Post-Pandemic

At the time of writing, the pandemic has raged on into its third year. Happy New Year! We are now in June 2023, my eldest son has just had COVID again. We were almost going to miss our Christmas, but he returned a negative result on 24 December.

This journey has been long and still feels somewhat relentless.

There has been an increasing amount of data based on overall mental health levels; this is a luxury we didn't have when the pandemic was brand new in March 2020. As the experts have consistently monitored mental health trends, we are aware that there has been a sharp increase in exhaustion, sleep disturbances, depression, and that the use of cannabis and alcohol abuse has increased. People were likely to self-medicate to cope with the pandemic.

Dr. Steven Sheris, Senior Vice President of Physician Enterprise at Atlantic Health and president of the Atlantic Medical Group, said 'We've all had COVID – whether or not we had the virus – because we've all been impacted emotionally. There's a subset of people who are manifesting as either behavioural issues or somatic body complaints that are a result of the COVID trauma, if not from the COVID virus itself'. Therefore, due to the consequences of COVID-19 such as social isolation, lower employment, and increased risk of debt, there are growing concerns about the sharp increase in mental health issues since the beginning of the pandemic.

The Effect of Lockdowns

'Lockdown' was a word humans rarely used until the 2020 COVID-19 pandemic; then it was all we could talk about. The pandemic had a fundamental impact on human lives, caused over one million deaths, and resulted in severe and unprecedented sanctions posed on our everyday life. These measures included schools closing, workplaces closing, people being made redundant, living rooms turned into home offices, and people being prohibited from seeing family and friends.

The social and emotional consequences of these restrictions are severe, and that's without the physical impact of a deadly virus to throw in the mix.

Understanding the impact of COVID-19 and lockdowns on happiness and wellbeing is difficult, purely because the research is still so new – only a year old – and because a lot of countries are still battling through the pandemic, in one way or another.

Some studies suggest that the pandemic has really impacted on overall happiness, particularly due to the isolating effects of lockdown, which exacerbated the cracks in relationships, partnerships, families, and friendships.

This is much worse for people who suffered financial setbacks during COVID-19, such as being made redundant or closing their business. Worrying about money and bills raises stress levels in the body, and this is why it is so important to ensure that the government is properly supporting people's livelihoods and incomes during these troubling times.

Overall happiness seems to increase once a lockdown is lifted in a country, reinforcing that humans are primarily social creatures who thrive from contact with each other. This is also confirmed by the fact that loneliness was the biggest factor in unhappiness during the pandemic. Adults who reported feeling lonely were most likely to register themselves as feeling unhappy.

Lockdown also highlighted the gap between the different socio-economic statuses. Those living below the poverty line suffered, especially for being unable to afford technology to complete online schoolwork etc.

What is Loneliness?

Prior to the pandemic, 20% of people identified as 'often feeling lonely'. Loneliness is a subjective feeling; for one person, being alone on a Friday night with a sad movie and a bottle of wine is their idea of heaven, whereas for another person it's their worst nightmare. Some people are comfortable going for dinner or to the cinema by themselves, others would never be seen dead asking for a movie ticket for one.

You may be surrounded by cheerful friends, a loving family, and a fulfilling relationship – yet you yearn for children and feel lonely without any babies in your arms. Therefore, everyone has a different idea of what loneliness is, and that is normal and not to be a comparison – if somebody confides in you about feelings of loneliness, don't remind them of the soiree they attended last night, or the dinner plans they have for next week.

Loneliness is a feeling of isolation causing feelings of sadness, rejection, jealousy, depression, and yearning for quality human contact. It is primarily caused by the absence of appropriate human contact, and can be caused by major life events, such as bereavement, transition, retirement, moving house … and pandemics. Remember that loneliness can affect people of all ages and all walks of life, particularly during a pandemic when lots of different groups of people will be experiencing distressing isolation.

Isolation doesn't always equal loneliness. In fact, some people feel totally satisfied not having to see anyone or make any plans. However, rather than presuming, it is important to check in with friends who are isolating. The feeling of loneliness is a complex emotion and experience.

How to Cope with Isolation and Loneliness

Calling a friend or someone who has COVID to check in increases a sense of connectedness. Take food, cook meals, and give toiletries to support those isolated. It will help them remember they are thought of and take the pressure off while they are caring for others or unwell. This habit of caring was seen to continue after the COVID-19 restrictions lifted and is a warm reminder of how supportive humans can be of one another.

Within lockdown, an easy area to begin to get your life back on track could be health and fitness. If you make a 1% change every day, which is miniscule, you'll be 100% transformed in no time if you have the patience and determination to stick at it. How many failed New Year's resolutions have you struggled to stick to? Think of the pandemic and lockdown as a forced reset for fitness and health; use it to discover a new indoor and outdoor exercise or download a fitness app, which can support you to achieve your new fitness goals.

Interestingly, the pandemic raised happiness levels in other areas of people's lives. As people adjusted to 'the new normal', it was clear that some of the changes in life were embraced positively.

Firstly, people rediscovered the neighbourly spirit of their community and neighbours, through small communities pulling together to support each other during the pandemic. This raised everybody's sense of togetherness and resilience.

People over the age of 60 reported feeling less lonely; this may seem counterintuitive because of the lockdown, however, relatives were phoning and video calling more than ever to 'check in'. Families were forced to find creative ways to bond, such as Zoom quizzes, and this increased overall relationship satisfaction.

3
AGORAPHOBIA AND SOCIAL ANXIETY

Agoraphobia

Agoraphobia is the debilitating, life limiting panic disorder that involves an extreme and irrational fear of being unable to face a certain place or situation, often manifesting in the sufferer being unable to leave their own home as the anxiety of the unfamiliar place is so overwhelming.

For the agoraphobic, home becomes their safe haven; it is an environment that is completely controllable, whereas the outside world is full of uncontrollable threats. Fear prevents the sufferer from entering the world; however, it is a vicious circle, because in avoiding facing their fears in the outside world, they spiral out of control and the agoraphobe becomes even more introverted and reclusive.

A person with agoraphobia may experience heart palpitations, sweating, tremors, rapid breathing, and chest pain, which could culminate in a full-blown anxiety attack, bringing on feelings of dying, losing control, and a distortion of reality. These feelings are commonly triggered in the outside world, in crowds, on public transport, and in enclosed spaces such as shops and restaurants. Worldwide lockdowns, in which government officials explicitly forbade people from going outside in certain contexts and situations created an environment for a panic disorder to develop.

While many people feel overjoyed as restrictions lift, people with agoraphobia feel even more anxious due to the strict quarantine measures that were in place. Also, before the pandemic, the fear of crowded public spaces could have been seen as irrational – however, now there is a deadly virus circulating, the fear is a reality and is entirely rational.

Overall Social Anxiety

Fear is a completely normal human emotion. It serves a purpose – when we were cave - people, the adrenaline fear provided propelled us away from danger. The threat response fear provides alerts us to unsafe situations. However, thanks to the pandemic, humans may feel a sense of fear over perfectly normal activities such as seeing friends, family, or visiting shared public spaces – which may escalate into social anxiety.

The difference between a sense of fear or worry and the psychological condition of social anxiety is the visceral reactions that happen in your body. Generalised fear and worry live in your head – your thoughts race, you imagine nightmare scenarios, you may even have nightmares. These are all processes that begin in the brain and stay in the brain. However, when this escalates into a psychological condition of anxiety, brain-based fear travels down into your body and causes physical reactions. Your foot may tap uncontrollably, your palms may become hot and sweaty, you may even throw up due to anxiety causing waves of nausea. This is a sign that the worry has gone beyond normal limitations, and it is time to seek professional help.

Social anxiety can be exacerbated by quarantine. During lockdown, there were social restrictions in place – however, this is not the same as quarantining, which is altogether stricter. Normally put in place when you have been in contact with or infected by COVID-19, quarantine involves isolating yourself from all human contact – not even accepting mail or food deliveries. This extreme isolation is not natural to humans, as we are a social species. Although it is important to prevent the spread of COVID-19, it can be very detrimental to mental health, especially for those living alone.

How the Pandemic Has Fueled Anxiety Disorders

During the pandemic, overall levels of diagnosed social anxiety increased (Thompson Mancebo & Moitra 2021). This was because people's sense of safety was threatened by the pandemic; physical interaction was discouraged, and new patterns of behaviour were established, such as not sitting near people on public transport and not sharing elevators.

Important opportunities for social contact were disrupted, and as a society we grew collectively more introverted. Meanwhile, all of this was actively encouraged by government messaging consistently warning us of impending death and illness if we socialised too much.

In many cases, the anxiety surrounding COVID-19 caused people to:
- worry about the spread of the virus, checking the news constantly for updates on statistics
- allow their fear to dictate changes in plans for work, family and friends
- imagine worst-case scenario outcomes
- feel 'on edge' throughout the day

A study conducted for *The Lancet* illustrated the rise of anxiety disorders, with a 25% increase of diagnosed anxiety worldwide, and a 27% increase of diagnosed depression (Santomauro 2021).

Coping Techniques for Agoraphobia and Social Anxiety in the Pandemic

Responses to returning to social situations such as work, weddings, restaurants, bars, and more will differ for each person. Even for an individual, their feelings may change day by day; one day, they feel reassured enough to go out for dinner, and then the next day they may feel anxious again due to a spike in COVID cases. All of this is normal in this context.

To work through these anxieties, visualise the upcoming event that is making you feel worried. Now, pinpoint the exact point that an upcoming interaction would trigger your anxiety. Would it be standing in line for a coffee and hearing the person behind you cough and sneeze on you without a mask on? Would it be going out for dinner and having the anxiety about asking people to do a RAT or PCR test beforehand, in case they judge you?

Whatever it is that triggers your fear response, strategise different methods to change the outcome in your mind and then visualise it all going smoothly. The power of visualisation is so important for managing anxiety – instead of telling yourself *it's all going to go wrong*, ask yourself: *but what if it all goes right?* Visualise yourself in society; healthy, happy, mixing with people, and being the most confident version of yourself.

In addition, be equipped with as much information as possible. There are going to be events that are out of your comfort zone, and that's okay, because if you take it too far too soon, you will overwhelm yourself and then be back at square one. Are you comfortable attending a wedding of 50, not 100? Maybe 100, but not 250? Understand your boundaries, provided they are within reason, and then gather the information you need to make an informed decision about whether the event is suitable for you or not. There is nothing worse than suffering with anxiety and being blindsided into an unbearable situation.

Be honest and speak your truth. Have honest conversations with your friends where you clearly outline your boundaries in a loving but firm way. If you are not comfortable hanging out without masks, let this be known. If you are not comfortable meeting up in groups of more than five, tell everybody in advance. This will take a lot of bravery and courage, because you may be disagreeing with a friend's belief. However, try and put away the feelings of being shy or fearful of being misunderstood. Expressing yourself and your boundaries is key.

Finally, if you are having repeated panic attacks – severe, physical reactions to intense fear causing shortness of breath, dizziness, a sense of doom, sweating, and more – then it is a sign you should seek professional help immediately. In addition, seek help if your anxiety is persistent – for example, from the moment you wake up to the moment you put your head on the pillow at night. Finally, if your fear is affecting your life functions – for example, not leaving the house, not going to the grocery store, not visiting friends – it is time to seek professional help.

This book is not a replacement for traditional therapy, counselling, cognitive behavioural therapy, or medicated interventions. These should be prescribed by a medical practitioner or counsellor. However, these techniques have worked for some people facing post pandemic anxiety, so it is always worth talking to your trusted medical and mental health professional for their advice on how to move forward.

4
THE IMPACT OF SCHOOL CLOSURES ON WELLBEING

The scale of COVID-19 as a modern pandemic was unpredictable. Its impacts on education were severe and disruptive and will be ongoing. However, some sources have identified the pandemic as a positive opportunity to 'reimagine, revitalize education' (United Nations 2021a).

Many schools around the world settled back into a 'blended learning' approach, with the impending threat of further lockdowns looming over the educational horizon.

Blended learning attempts to combine in-person teaching and online delivery, giving students access to the classroom environment remotely and in the school setting (Concannon 2005). As a result, students have been both onsite and offsite, online and offline, in a purgatory state of coming and going between academic sites.

Researchers have noted that online learning can be engaging and active, suggesting that remote learning can produce equal educational outcomes to traditional delivery with the right tools and methods (Bernard, Abrami & Lou 2004).

Effect on Students

School closures were experienced worldwide in the battle to win against the virus. Multiple children lost around two years of learning time; two years of changed exam conditions, online learning, and vital school experiences taken away from them, such as high school graduations, dances, or proms.

In addition to learning time, school provides a wide range of socio-emotional development such as making friends, managing conflict, and learning teamwork and communication skills. This loss is more keenly felt in younger children; they missed out on social skills that prepare them for their first years at school.

Many schools reverted to home learning during lockdown, sending out tasks and homework for children to do under parental supervision. This was met with mixed reviews; a home environment could not truly replace a school environment with a qualified teacher, especially if the home environment was unstable or abusive.

Furthermore, at times parents were expected to support the schoolwork, especially with younger children. This placed emotional strain on the parents, some of whom don't have a high level of education, and created tension between the student, teacher, and parents.

Effect on Parents

In a study conducted across Europe, many parents felt unsatisfied with home learning and home-schooling. They did not agree that it provided the same quality education as regular school, and that schools were not able to provide enough support when there was a topic unfamiliar to parents. This was especially exacerbated by families who had younger children; most likely due to the demanding nature of younger children, and the extra support they would need with home-schooling and following a home learning timetable.

Parents with older teenagers generally reported fewer signs of anxiety and a lower impact on 'normal' life as the children were old enough to complete their tasks independently (Thorell Skoglund & de la Peña 2021).

Isolation was not good for young people's mental health as it reduced face to face contact with peers and reduced incidental or planned recreational exercise, an issue for both health and wellbeing.

In addition, a lot of parents and carers struggled to maintain regular contact with the teacher, as they were no longer able to speak to them face to face at school. This caused an increase in stress and domestic arguments within the family, impacting the family's wellbeing.

Rosamund McNeil, president of the National Education Union, stated that 'Parents aren't – and don't have to be – teachers. They don't have to achieve everything a teacher would. They should do what they can to try to help their child access the learning schools have set, but they have to be realistic' (Ferguson 2021).I found working and home-schooling a difficult juggle, not one I hope too ever do again.

Alternatively, lockdown presented an interesting opportunity for some parents who fully embraced and enjoyed home-schooling; these included children who were bullied at school or found school a stressor on mental health, children who find following the school routine difficult, and parents who reported having highly stressful jobs that took away from their family time.

Effect on Education

Before the pandemic, three million children worldwide were home-schooled, with the majority being based in the USA, UK, Canada, New Zealand, and Australia. In some countries, such as Germany and Greece, it is completely illegal, whereas in other countries, such as Russia, it is legal but subject to strict rules and regulations.

However, due to the pandemic forcing more than 168 million children to miss school for a full year or more (UNICEF 2021), schools were forced to think of creative ways to encourage learning at home.

One in seven children missed more than 75% of their total face-to-face learning. There is no research yet as to how this has impacted children in meeting their developmental milestones.

Henrietta Fore, the Executive Director of UNICEF, said 'As we approach the one - year mark of the COVID-19 pandemic, we are again reminded of the catastrophic education emergency worldwide lockdowns have created. With every day that goes by, children unable to access in-person schooling fall further and further behind, with the most marginalized paying the heaviest price' (United Nations 2021b).

By 'most marginalized', Fore means those living in 'digital poverty', unable to afford the technology needed for the digital shift in education the pandemic caused. Being able to afford modern technology that works quickly and accurately is a luxury for the privileged that many take for granted. It allowed many students to access online classes, download homework and stay in communication with their teachers.

However, for the 40% of the world that do not have access to the internet (The World Bank 2020), it created an even bigger divide in equality and left millions of children unable to access their learning. Therefore, poorer children were more likely to eventually return to school even further behind their peers who were able to access the internet.

In addition, the requirements for parents to become both home educators and home workers, as well as take care of the home, manage bills, and feed their families put great strain on their mental wellbeing. Some parents found it very difficult to motivate their children, as children had not adapted to parents becoming teachers, and struggled to listen to their parent's advice.

If you are a parent experiencing uncertainty over your abilities, doubts, and fears that you can provide the best learning experience possible for your child, the most important thing to remember is to take care of yourself. On planes, you should always put on your own oxygen masks before tending to your child's, and it is the same with home-schooling. You can only support your child's learning if you are feeling well in yourself and calm.

Dedicate time to yourself every single day by walking, having a long hot bath, or calling a friend to offload your problems. Remember that children learn by observation, and if they see you being calm and positive, they are likely to react in a calm and peaceful way. And vice versa – if you are negative about home learning, your child is likely to model your behavior.

5

THE SOCIETAL DIVIDE

Although the same virus spread around the world, COVID-19 had dramatically different effects for different groups of people.

The virus thrives on inequality, not just weakened immune systems. It is no secret that the poorest, less developed parts of the world were hit the hardest, through no fault of their own. People around the world without guaranteed healthcare, such as those in the United States, faced a much higher likelihood of disease, complications, and death. In addition, those living in less wealthy economies also faced hardships. The pandemic sharply decreased global income with a rise in poor people across all areas of the world.

However, the real marker of the poverty divide is the ability to bounce back from poverty. The poorest 40% of people most affected by COVID-19 may not have recovered their financial losses; however, the top 40% of earners not only recovered their losses but have already earned more. This is because wealthy people were able to return from furlough to their high-paying jobs, whereas those in true poverty were left deeper in the cycle than ever before.

A positive case study to focus on is how New Zealand handled the pandemic. A small island with just over 5 million inhabitants trusted their then prime minister, Jacinda Ardern. The government was highly transparent and stood in solidarity with its citizens. The people of New Zealand expect a high level of social justice and are therefore prepared to make difficult decisions and restrict their own freedoms for the good of others. They are also highly compliant and guided by the science, with a high uptake of the vaccine.

In addition, with smart and fast-acting political decisions, such as immediately shutting borders, New Zealand quickly and effectively brought the disease under control. New Zealand did not have a divided society – they had a united society. All other countries can see New Zealand as an example of hope, teamwork, and the power of being together.

Restarting Our Communication as a Society

Our interpretation of facial expression, social cues and body language has certainly suffered. Due to the mask usage, social distancing, and personal protective equipment (PPE), interpersonal communication skills have suffered.

Communication has been stifled – our words muffled by masks, our facial expressions distorted by PPE, not to mention the profound difficulty it causes people with special needs, particularly those who rely on lipreading to communicate.

Nonverbal communication, which includes facial gestures, expressions, body language, and hand signals, makes up 55% of all forms of human communication, therefore PPE poses a huge restriction on communication (Mohammadi 2021).

While keeping in mind the medical requirements for keeping the pandemic at bay, there are a number of strategies that can be employed to restart our communication as a society. The use of body language needs to be emphasised. For example, make sure you are directly turned towards the person speaking to you, and pay full attention to what is being communicated, especially if the person has hearing loss. Hand gestures can be increased. Although not a full substitute for clear verbal communication, any form of emphasised body language is better than nothing.

Additionally, use of digital technology – such as Zoom, Skype, and other platforms – should be used where possible, so that communication can be as visual as possible without being restricted by PPE. Finally, it is very important that people are aware of the communication difficulties that can be caused by PPE, particularly for people with special needs or barriers to communication. Therefore, clear masks should be used to enable hearing-enabled people to lip read.

The Vaccination Divide

To vax, or not to vax – that is the question could be a modern twist on a famous Shakespearean quote. Vaccination was on everybody's lips – it was all anybody could talk about. Some countries offered privileges to the vaccinated, such as attending concerts, holidays, restaurants, and nightclubs. These people were able to socialise at a much earlier rate than the unvaccinated, giving them mental health benefits by reducing their risk of depression and anxiety a lot earlier.

It also affected the nation economically – those who were vaccinated were able to return to work earlier and with a reduced likelihood of illness, meaning they were able to earn more, relieving the financial burden. The unvaccinated were further at risk of furlough, redundancy, or illness, preventing them from working and leading to a higher likelihood of financial hardship.

As not everybody in society will be vaccinated for a myriad of reasons, this sense of 'freedom' for a few, not all, led to resentment, unrest, and downright rebellion from the marginalised few.

In addition, it caused huge conflict within society – the great debate continues to rage on both online and offline – damaging relationships between families, friends, and couples.

If you are struggling to communicate with a loved one due to differing opinions on the vaccine, there are a few things to question. Firstly, is the source you are debating over reliable? Is it a scientific, evidence-based piece of research, or is it merely gossip? Is this debate showing empathy and compassion for each other's views, or is it resorting to insults and personal attacks?

Debates are healthy, but they should always be respectable and never cross the line into insulting. Remember that there is a time and a place for a spirited debate, and if alcohol is involved, it probably isn't the best solution for clear communication. If these basic requirements are not met, the barriers in communication will grow wider than ever before.

6

LOCKDOWN FATIGUE

Lockdown fatigue is a new term used to describe the extreme exhaustion caused by the pandemic. This manifests itself in different ways in our everyday tasks, our work, and our social circles.

Many people feel lethargic and drained by the simple tasks that we used to take for granted, such as meeting friends for a coffee. For key workers such as medical professionals, their jobs were twice as hard both physically and mentally. Many people reported they were too tired to arrange social events – they want to connect with others but have little energy to do so.

Physical fatigue

The stress of the pandemic disrupted sleeping patterns all around the world. Restless nights lead to exhaustion, which leads to an overabsorption of caffeine, which leads to crashing lows, further compounding the exhaustion.

Some people who become infected with COVID-19 suffer from long COVID, with periods of extreme fatigue, exhaustion, and 'brain fog', where you are too exhausted to think properly. This is an experience many of my patients, family, and friends have talked about.

Emotional fatigue

Some people are feeling fatigued by the new hoops we must jump through to do the normal, everyday tasks we used to do easily.

In the new normal, tasks such as getting vaccinated for a concert, taking a COVID test before meeting friends, and constantly sanitising your hands can be overwhelmingly complicated. Things we just used to do without thinking now require an extra step and planning, such as booking a COVID test to go on holiday. Although these extra measures keep us safe, it can be draining having to jump through hoops for a simple task or event.

How to Reduce Lockdown Fatigue After Lockdown

Pushing back against lockdown fatigue involves being active in a way that's right for you – for some people that may look like walking, a light jog, or simply just going out to sit in the fresh air.

Vitamin D is vital, particularly in winter. Although natural sources are best, if you are not able to get out into the sunshine, consider supplemental forms of vitamin D.

Although this may sound contrary, *reducing* your caffeine and sugar levels will power you through the slump. Caffeine and sugar provide a temporary boost, but the crash will leave you more fatigued than when you started.

Fatigue can often be caused by a lack of structure, so to reduce the brain fog, make sure you have the same bedtime and wake up time every single day.

Follow the same routine daily to give yourself some structure, and if the pandemic has completely turned your structure on its head, then create the new one of your dreams. Add in some reading, some meditation, gratitude practice – take control of your day.

Before bedtime, avoid devices that emit blue light – no more late-night scrolling! Blue light will stimulate the brain, rather than allowing it to switch off and relax. I noticed physical signs of stress in my jaw and head.

Check your stress levels and your body's natural signals that your stress levels are rising. Is your jaw clenched? Shoulders hunched? Any nervous tapping of the foot or hands? Legs jiggling? Many issues may be causing your stress, such as vulnerable family members or financial issues, but stress makes you feel exhausted by the meteoric rising of cortisol levels. To stay calm and reduce fatigue, incorporate journaling into your morning and evening routine.

7

COLLECTIVE SOCIAL ANGER

Alongside fear, anger is a primitive emotion that has kept us safe over millions of years. Megan Hays, clinical psychologist at the University of Alabama, says 'Anger is an emotion, not a behaviour. Anger tells us that something isn't right. Perhaps our safety is being threatened, injustice is happening, or some action is being required of us.

If no one had felt anger about the pandemic, we may never have developed vaccines or instituted masking and distancing requirements, because no one would care what happened to the people around them' (Hoge 2021).

Recently, society has turned its anger and rage towards an inevitable force – the pandemic. Anger at the government, anger at the vaccinations, anger at the restrictions, anger at other people.

Irritability is a common reaction to stress, and there are multiple factors of the pandemic that may be stressing you out, either silently or obviously. Tiny inconveniences such as long queues due to social distancing seem to trigger an irrational wave of anger.

'COVID anger' or 'pandemic anger', the ongoing frustration and rage at a situation that's out of our control, is a very normal emotion for humans to be experiencing right now.

Anger is a perfectly rational part of the coping process; as a society, we have been robbed of so many moments, memories, and experiences that should have been ours to enjoy. Along with economic downturns and social injustice, anger is inevitable during these turbulent times. In fact, anger, when used correctly, can be a productive and stimulating emotion that forces us into action.

The Use of Media to Advertise Anger

In these times, it feels like anger is almost inevitable. We are constantly reminded of the shortcomings of the world and the pandemic from the news, the media, our conversations, our work colleagues. It seems that the media is everywhere, and it fills the air with a negative buzz that weighs heavy on our shoulders.

Social media has a lot to answer for. Declining mental health, especially in the younger generations, has been attributed to the increase of social media and screen time. An interesting finding from research showed the overuse of social media has led to increased weight gain, disrupted sleep patterns, impaired memory function, and withdrawal from society (Small et al 2020).

Mass hysteria has been fuelled by social media. Pictures of empty shelves at the grocery store circulated, the media reported food shortages, and misinformation spread like wildfire. When the virus was brand new, even top scientists were being challenged by the symptoms, the rate it spreads, how it spreads, and false information spread through the internet and infected users with hysteria.

How to Reduce Anger During and After COVID-19 and Restore Balance

Anger becomes unhealthy when it derails you from achieving your goals and converts into aggressive, spiteful behaviour. If you feel like pandemic anger is blocking you from achieving your potential or making a difficult time worse, try moving away and focusing less on things that trigger it such as switching off social media and stepping away from the screens until your heart rate slows and you can take deep breaths.

Make sure you have a good balance in your life – often, irritability and snappiness are a sign that we are neglecting our self-care needs, and that we are directing our energy towards negative outlets. Also, recognise when you need time to yourself, away from the expectations of family, work, the media, and your social life. Time to yourself is precious for rejuvenating energy and perspective.

Understand the difference between responding to anger and reacting angrily. When you acknowledge and respond to anger, you notice your anger cues in your body, when they start – the increase heart rate, rise in temperature, tension, the vein pulsating in your temple, the clenched teeth, the raised voice.

You recognise it, you understand that you are reaching breaking point, but you still have the cognitive and emotional capacity to step away from the situation and process what you are feeling. This is regulating your emotions and responding not reacting.

Alternatively, when you react angrily, it results in 'snapping', reacting in a split-second, often verbally or physically, saying things you don't mean and taking action that you immediately regret.

If you do find yourself losing your cool too often, consider increasing your physical exercise i.e. go walking, running, cycling, punch a punching bag, jumping up and down stairs – if that's not enough, up the ante to more physical sports, such as contact sports or martial arts. These can be a perfect outlet for physical frustration, while blowing off some steam and increasing the endorphins that flow through your body and melt the stress away.

8

THE POWER OF FEAR

As COVID -19 spread around the world, fear rippled through every country. Fear infected millions of people, spread by the media, causing erratic and unpredictable behaviour such as rioting, protests, panic buying, and economic downturn.

Just as anger is a perfectly valid human emotion, fear is a normal response to the danger that the pandemic posed. If you had not experienced COVID-19, you may still feel fear for loved ones, the fate of the country, and what the future may hold.

When a society is reacting based on fear, they become ruled by their emotions, and logic and reason take a backseat. Poor decisions are made, such as arguing with strangers on the internet, people telling people how to park their trolleys in the supermarket car park trolley bay (this happened to me), people yelling at people waiting for their kids in their car (this also happened to me and other mum's at our school pickup), as one or neither party cannot rationally handle the facts that have been given to them.

'It is tempting to dismiss these fears as the expression of an emotional overreaction. On the contrary, they signal the existence of profound uncertainties experienced by people who are having to make several difficult decisions' (Pelissolo et al 2020). The presence of fear during the pandemic triggers an innate defensive response that dates back to the beginning of humankind.

These defensive feelings are continuing today and there are reports of people acting defensively outside their window of tolerance. Defensive fight or flight behaviours are triggered in survival situations, a natural response to an imminent threat.

How to Reduce Lockdown Fear and Find Your Inner Strength

Studies have shown that fear of COVID and the severity of COVID can be prevented by financial support, medical assistance, a cautious attitude towards the media, and a positive attitude towards reduced social contact (Coelho 2020).

However, as you approach the return to normal life, make sure that you take it at your own pace. If your friends are happy enough to return to a venues such as nightclubs or the movies, that may not be well ventilated but you aren't ready, have the courage to say no. Make sure that you are taking small steps towards being a social being again.

While it's hard after we have been so isolated, build yourself up to small social events such as going for coffee with people you feel comfortable with. There is no right way to re-enter the new normal world.

In addition, if you believe that too many media outlets have infiltrated your brain, consider giving a trusted friend your communication devices to give yourself a well-earned break from social media.

Reframing is an important concept during the pandemic. Negative cycles of thought, often generated by the endless cycles of restrictions and lockdown, can generate feelings of fear and anxiety.

When you catch yourself spiralling into negativity, you can use this to recognise the feelings you are experiencing and reframe them in a positive way. For example, if you are worried you are going to lose your job or anxious to go to school, change the thoughts to a positive one. You can do this. Try and find one or two positive thoughts 'I can do this' or 'I am ok'.

Try and think of something you are grateful for. You might need some prompting. Look at the sky, the ocean, a beautiful plant, enjoy a book, smell a flower, and look at a photo of a good memory, hugging a good friend, playing with your dog or cat, in my case swimming, and walking my horse, a time you enjoyed a delicious meal, a time you laughed so hard you cried. There is always something even small.

9

THE IMPACT OF UNEMPLOYMENT

Tackling the mental health impact of unemployment or loss of business due to the COVID-19 pandemic will be difficult, and it will take years of ongoing work. Losing a job is a turbulent life event and can cause feelings of trauma if not dealt with effectively.

Financial insecurity is a massive risk factor for mental health issues, and during the pandemic the mental health of unemployed people measured significantly worse than those working from home or key workers' mental health (OECD 2021).

Combined with how stretched mental health services were feeling before the pandemic, COVID-19 came at the worst possible time. Many adults reported an increase in anxiety, depression, and sadness during the pandemic due to loss of work and change in routine.

Impact of Unemployment on Mental Wellbeing

Does work make you happy and give you a purpose? If so, how much does your work affect your happiness levels? A lot of us spend more time at work than we do at home, and more time with our co-workers than we do our own family members.

If you are self-employed; the lack of colleagues and co-workers can lower the social aspect of working and cause sadness or loneliness. In addition, people who are self-employed may feel higher levels of anxiety, due to the instability of their work.

Ultimately, whether you're employed or self-employed, having no employment is a clear indicator of low wellbeing. Having a job is more than just an income; it's a sense of purpose, a reason to get up in the morning.

People who are employed rank the value of their life and happiness a lot higher than those who are unemployed, showing that unemployment has a way of 'embedding' itself into someone's personality, until they adapt being unemployed as a reflection of themselves. It reflects poorly on their social status, social relationships, daily routine, and long-term achievements, all of which contribute to happiness levels.

Employers have a moral duty to support the mental health of their employees during the pandemic, particularly in industries heavily affected by the pandemic, such as hospitality, health, or education.

One action that employers can take is to not completely sever a contract with a former employee during the pandemic, but rather place them on a 'furlough' or 'retention' scheme, meaning their job position is still open for them once the pandemic has settled down. Workers who were guaranteed their jobs eventually reported no increase at all in mental health issues, depression, or anxiety, as their financial situation would balance out (Smith et al 2020).

Rediscovering Your Life Purpose

Many people have launched from panicking in a pandemic to pursuing their life purpose or finding new passions. It is not an easy transition to make. The pandemic turned the world completely upside down, and as we embraced 'the new normal', many of us pivoted in our personal lives and completely changed our realities.

We changed relationships, careers, housing, hobbies. When the world was in crisis, we rose from the ashes and found new identities, talents, and purpose. The virus may have challenged us to redefine our future; it exposed all the cracks in our lives and forced us to consider them. Relationships broke up, arguments were caused, houses were moved out of.

While others were feeling disoriented and lazy, the proactive pandemic members hustled and worked hard, even if they were laid off from their original job. But how do these people know what their purpose is?

The trick is to expand your horizons literary. Find autobiographies of people you admire – people with passion, wealthy business people, pillars of our society, successful women and men, tech experts – and then read like your life depends on it.

It's also important to find your community, with similar goals – if your goal is to have zero debt, buddy up with someone you know who is on a debt journey themselves. If your goal during the pandemic is to lose weight, find an exercise buddy. Being able to talk to somebody who truly understands what your goals are will feel like a weight is lifted off your shoulders.

10

WORK, OVERWORKING, AND KEY WORKERS

During lockdown, many 'essential' services continued, such as firefighters, the police service, medical professionals, retails workers, and many more. In fact, in many cases, their jobs became more complex and emotionally and physically demanding. Dressed in full PPE, key workers worked throughout the pandemic to provide the same level of service as pre-pandemic.

In general, key workers – particularly medical professionals – are more disposed to anxiety, burnout, and lack of sleep compared to other professions (West et al 2018).

Some of these key workers were eventually diagnosed with anxiety, depression, and, in severe cases, PTSD (Rodríguez-Rey 2020). This was the result of having to cope with the stress of the pandemic and the toll on loved ones, as well as an already stressful career to begin with, making them vulnerable to emotional distress.

Those on the front line of the pandemic are said to grade themselves as more highly distressed than those working from home (González-Sanguine 2020).

Overworking: The Silent Killer

Overworking is a silent killer. During the pandemic, many professions quoted a weekly average of six hours more work than normal, suggesting the pandemic increased workload and stress levels (Rodríguez-Rey, Rocio et al 2020).

Even before the pandemic, the predicted levels of death by overworking were 750,000 a year (Ro 2021). This is more than the global statistics for those dying from malaria.

Due to short deadlines, strict budgets, and never-ending to-do lists, long working hours – defined as 55 hours of work or more a week – can drastically reduce your life expectancy.

In fact, overworking is the biggest risk factor for work-related illness and disease. Overworking can lead to an increase in chronic stress, blood pressure, and cholesterol, which increases your likelihood of a heart attack.

Additionally, if you are overworking, you are likely to be sleeping less and exercising less, as well as eating more comfort or convenience foods. All of this leads to weight gain and strain on the heart.

Overworking is not just exhausting, it's a killer. Overworking affects different groups of people in different ways. Normally, men tend to overwork more the women, especially middle-aged men. Some countries are more proactive than others – for example, in the European Union, employees are banned from working more than 48 hours a week.

Overworking hours grew exponentially through the pandemic, and if the trend continues, key workers will become unhealthier and more unhappy. Self-care is so important to reduce stress.

The Glorification of Overworking

While the culture of overworking is booming, our mental health and physical capacity is declining. For many jobs, the work culture involves placing your work over everything – your family, friends, romantic life, and self-care. It becomes a vicious circle.

This is particularly true for key workers in the pandemic, who were continuously called upon to do extended hours of service for the good of the nation. Even retired teachers and medical professionals were asked to leave retirement and come back to service, despite often being older and more vulnerable.

If you find that you are stuck in a cycle of overworking with no feasible way out, remind yourself that there is no medal you receive for being the last car left in the car park, or the last person to log off your computer.

In fact, overworking will make you feel bitter and spiteful; you'll compare your achievements to those who work less hours than you, and secretly hope they aren't favoured as highly as you. If they get a promotion, rather than being pleased for your colleague, you'll think, *but they leave at 4:30pm every day! It's not fair. I stay until past 6!* And that is not beneficial for your wellbeing.

Instead, it's time to have a frank and honest conversation with yourself and your loved ones. Ask your trusted friends and family: *Do I overwork? Am I present?* The answer may likely be no, and it may hurt to hear, but you must listen.

Once you have accepted that you are overworked and it is affecting your personal life, it's time to draw some healthy boundaries. By understanding what to say no to and having strict rules about it – e.g. 'I will leave work early on a Thursday to take my children swimming' – you can establish a set of non-negotiables that will make your workday more bearable.

This is something I have started doing; I have changed my working calendar to reflect fifteen face to face client hours a week and will no longer work four to five days a week.

Imposter Syndrome During the Pandemic

Imposter syndrome is a feeling of inadequacy for normally work-related tasks, where you become riddled with anxiety at the feeling that eventually you will be 'found out' and someone will uncover that you are not as good as you believe.

The pandemic has transitioned so many of our job roles that we previously felt 'safe' in – for example, a comfortable office job – to a fully remote, home working role where you are also expected to home-school young children. Therefore, it's easy to appreciate that some work tasks we have previously been expert at, we are now out of our depth in.

And while you are floundering and flustered, trying to figure everything out, on Instagram your co-worker seems to be giving off the appearance that life is a breeze – her children are dressed, ready for the day, eating a fresh home-cooked breakfast while she's already made three sales by 9am.

When we feel tidal waves of self-doubt and that there are other people doing their jobs better than us, it can trigger a feeling of imposter syndrome, where you believe that you're not as smart, hardworking, sociable, talented, as you think yourself to be, and that any minute somebody will call you out. Imposter syndrome is actually due to the threat response our body and psychology is facing during the pandemic.

If you hear a voice in your head telling you that you are not enough, that you are undeserving of an accolade and everybody is going to find out you're a fraud, silence that voice in your head by. Remind yourself of the genuine achievements you have accomplished. Facts don't lie; whether you are convincing yourself you deserved it or not, you received that award/title/honour.

Put a positive spin on your imposter syndrome – if you were staying in your comfort zone and playing it safe, you wouldn't be hearing that niggling voice of self-doubt. It's a sign you're advancing on to bigger and better things; so, tell the voice thanks, but no thanks.

11

BEREAVEMENT AND LOSS

At the time of writing, the officially recorded COVID-19 death toll is 5.5 million and counting. Those who lost a loved one during COVID-19 experienced bereavement in the most tragic way possible; one of the few times in human history where mourners were not allowed to be hugged or visited with flowers. Instead, the bereaved were locked in isolation. Cards posted through the door just aren't the same.

This lack of emotional support, bonding, and love can make the bereaved feel alone and isolated, which is a dangerous combination when mixed with the wide range of emotions that grief brings.

Furthermore, due to the nature of the virus that took so many lives, many people didn't get the chance to say goodbye and to begin the healing process. As the virus was so infectious, loved ones were not able to visit the hospital or to hold the hands of the dying. This can cause painful, traumatic feelings which, if not processed, can manifest into long-term guilt.

The World Health Organization estimates an 'excess mortality'; that is, the unofficial deaths of many millions more than the recorded figures. There are many reasons why experts believe that the estimated death toll for COVID-19 is much, much higher than the recorded death toll.

For example, many died before we had the facilities to test and treat for the virus. Deaths were labelled mistakenly as another illness, such as an asthma attack. Some who died from other ailments such as cancer, not from COVID-19, and the hospitals were possibly too busy and too full to give those patients the diagnosis and care they deserved. All routine lifesaving checks such as mammograms, cervical cancer smears, and prostate exams were all postponed, leading to a late diagnosis or none at all.

Our Grief Rituals

Grief rituals are any cultural process and procedure used to mark the death of a loved one. Every culture and religion celebrates life or commiserates death differently, and has done for millions of years – from Stone Age cremations to Egyptian embalming. Grief rituals are vital to a culture because the funeral is when the family can start to acknowledge the sadness of the passing and begin the journey to healing.

In the 21st century, COVID-19 has drastically altered the way we mourn our losses as a society. Our usual, traditional social rituals – such as attending funerals, wakes, and celebrating a life well lived – have been callously snatched away from us.

Described as adding 'a second layer of loss' (Watts 2021), the pandemic is keeping us from being physically together, and emotionally connected.

Worldwide, many places of worship closed their doors to religious burials. Even in non-religious funeral homes, funerals were limited to small numbers and live streamed to wider family and friends at home.

Despite the ability to live-stream a funeral, a feat of modern technology, this experience is made more bitter by the fact that it robs the grieving family of a safe outlet for their emotions and the comfort that the room is filled with loving members of family and friends. Instead of an outpouring of love and sympathy, this face-to-face contact has been replaced by texting and online messaging. It simply is no substitute for a warm hug and 'I'm sorry for your loss'.

After a substantial loss, these virtual actions are simply not enough; as humans, we crave physical touch, closeness, and affection, which we were starved of during the pandemic.

How Do You Cope with Grief During a Pandemic?

Isolated, alone, and grieving. It really could not get much worse for mourning during the pandemic. If you lost a loved one during the pandemic, I would like to express my condolences to you and I am sorry for your loss. Sadly, due to quarantine rules people were less likely to be able to express their grief in a healthy, productive manner.

If you are grieving, it is okay to have more than one remembrance ceremony – a virtual one, and an in-person ceremony when restrictions are lifted. It's important to discuss happy times, fond memories, bonding experiences, and to laugh and smile with one another amongst the grief. The sooner the better, even if held over Zoom.

If you are supporting a loved one who is grieving, if there are restrictions in place preventing you from physically seeing someone who you know is experiencing grief, phone them regularly to check in, and meet with them as soon as it is physically safe. They will appreciate the continued care and will know that you supported them in their darkest moments.

When you can finally meet in person, this can be days, weeks, months, maybe even a year after the loved one has passed. Although their stage in the healing process will have understandably progressed, this doesn't mean that they have forgotten all about the loss and gotten over it. Approach with compassion and a listening ear, ready to hear their story and feelings without judgement.

The inability to attend funerals during the pandemic was crushing for many. Attending a funeral is scientifically proven to be able to support adults and children through a grieving process, by providing essential social support to those who are experiencing a loss. It also supports the loved ones to move through the grieving process in a healthier, better way, rather than remaining stuck in one stage of grief (Burrell and Selman 2020).

Reimagining mourning during COVID-19 has led to some brilliantly creative yet utterly tragic ways of marking a loved ones passing.

Ultimately, the main emotion that will support you through this difficult time is acceptance. Accepting that the funeral will be different, the turnout will be different, the atmosphere will be different. However, it is your family's funeral, and you deserve inner peace, which comes from accepting the situation as it is, not comparing it to as it was.

Studies have shown that writing or telling stories about the deceased can ease the healing process when social restrictions are in place and therefore the bereaved have less social contact. This is likely because written posts on social media regarding the deceased are often met with an outpouring of love, releasing a serotonin hit when the poster acknowledges the comments and messages (Wagner et al 2006).

Therefore, if you are struggling at any point with feelings of grief, it may be worth expressing your emotions through the art of writing, whether digitally or the traditional form of journaling.

Above all, this guide is not intended as a replacement for therapy, although this actionable advice is certainly useful. If you are truly struggling to cope with grief, the best place to be is speaking to a qualified counsellor or therapist, particularly one trained for grief and bereavement counselling.

12

EXISTENTIAL CHANGE AND METAMORPHOSIS

Metamorphosis is a Greek term meaning the process of changing shape, also used to refer to a personal transformation from the inside out. Many species use the biological process of metamorphosis as they journey through life – most famously, caterpillars transforming into beautiful butterflies.

During the pandemic, many people and businesses had to adapt themselves and their lives to survive. Restaurants became takeaways, bars became drink delivery services, personal trainers ran outdoor sessions. When life throws an unpredictable event your way, it's important for your own mental clarity to make meaning of it.

Humans have an innate need to make sense of the unpredictability of life – that's why there is debate over how the earth was created, how the dinosaurs were wiped out, how Stonehenge was formed, and many other intricacies of life that we may never truly know.

The ability to adapt is valuable. Furthermore, if you don't make meaning of a traumatic event like the pandemic, grief and trauma can follow you wherever you go.

Those who fully embraced the change and process of metamorphosis ended up thriving, not just surviving. New ways of life emerged, with new, healthier routines established.

People who are agile run towards change, rather than away from it. If you feel like the pandemic has turned your life upside down, try to find things that you can embrace as a chance for positive change. You never know, you may just end up in a better position than you started and discover a new purpose and lease for life.

This is why it's called 'the new normal' – the old has been left behind, and the chance of a fresh start lies ahead. Embrace it, rather than dread it. If it feels overwhelming, break the old and new normal down into social life, work life, family life, health and wellbeing, spiritual life, creative needs, and other headings that you may find useful to review.

Discovering New Hobbies, New Purpose, and a New Life

The pandemic turned the world on its head – traditional hobbies and recreational activities, such as dining, drinking, sports, theatre, cinema, leisure, and socialising were cancelled.

As a result, many people took up new hobbies and activities, such as learning a language, bike riding, online gym sessions, online learning, walking, outdoor socialising, meeting neighbours at fence lines, walking the block, crafting, and charity work.

The benefits of a new hobby include a welcome distraction from the doom and gloom, as a new hobby provides an outlet for your frustration. In addition, the pandemic took so much away – weddings, funerals, livelihoods, education. Having a hobby is a way of giving back to yourself by providing important 'me time' to find a mode of comfort during difficult periods. In addition, hobbies force you to learn new skills and are a way of challenging yourself mentally and physically, supporting your transformation into the best version of yourself.

A survey of 2,000 adults in the UK concluded that over a third took up a new hobby during the pandemic, with the most popular pastimes being gardening, growing fruits and vegetables, cooking, and baking (Hughes 2021). Other options included walking, reading, biking riding, knitting, jumping on the trampoline, and outdoor exercise.

Many of these hobbies are easily accessible and improve your mental health while adding structure to an everyday routine.

It also keeps your mind busy and stops you from ruminating on negativity. Activities such as gardening and decorating also improve your living area, which is especially important for people who are temporarily not working during a pandemic. Overall, having a hobby or discovering a new one is an excellent way to take control of the uncontrollable, and put a positive spin on the situation.

Creative Outlets and Hobbies

Creative therapies and art can ease anxiety during COVID-19. It's no secret that the pandemic put more burden on so many of us already struggling with mental illness, such as anxiety and depression, and creative therapies can be an outlet for frustration.

Creative hobbies can help you regain a sense of control in an uncontrollable situation. Replacing sadness with inspiration can lift the spirits. Also, the feeling of being productive in a time of isolation, where people are typically more sedentary, is good for your mental health and wellbeing.

People engaging in creative arts to seek solace and the sensation of being in 'a flow state'. The flow sensation of being immersed in something creative, often losing track of time can be intensely joyful.

CONCLUSION

'The green reed which bends in the wind is stronger than the mighty oak which breaks in a storm.'

Confucius

This guide was written to support those who are struggling to cope with the short and long-term effects of COVID-19. While not attempting to replace any methods of therapy, I hope it brought to you sage and useful advice that you can embed throughout everyday life.

If there is one thing to take away from this guide, it would be this: speak up. No matter what you are feeling, find someone to confide in and speak to them about how you are feeling. Just having a listening ear to offload your problems can help relieve you of your worries and mental burden, no matter how heavy they are to carry.

And above all, be kind to yourself. Hopefully this pandemic is a once in a lifetime event – always remember you did the best you could at the time with what you were given, which wasn't an awful lot.

Don't get lost in the 'would have, could have, should have'– that would involve looking back in the past; you can't get where you want to be by going back there. Onwards and upwards from now on and focus on *Harnessing Your Wellness*.

ABOUT THE AUTHOR

Naomi is a registered psychologist who worked through the COVID-19 pandemic. In January 2022, she contracted COVID-19, as did her two sons and husband. These experiences prompted her to write this book.

Naomi has lived experience of a natural disaster – the 1995 Earthquake that rocked Japan. In 2009 Naomi joined the disaster recovery effort following the devastating bushfires in Victoria, working in recovery centres where she was contracted to write and facilitate a trauma sensitive experiential horse therapy program for those affected by the fires. She continues to work with horses in therapy.

Naomi has experience working in natural disaster recovery, trauma focused therapy, crisis management, child and family development and natural horsemanship. She has worked in educational institutions, local government, clinical mental health services, not-for-profit organisations, and private practice.

Naomi has a keen interest in ongoing research and support for mental health practitioners wanting to incorporate equine assisted therapy into clinical practice. Naomi offers supervision to practitioners who work with horses in therapy for people.

When the pandemic started in Australia in 2020, Naomi had to temporarily close the equine assisted therapy side of her business, but worked as a psychologist via telehealth and seeing people face to face when permitted. She reopened her equine assisted therapy practice in mid-late 2022.

Day to day, Naomi runs Harnessing Wellness Psychology, a private psychology practice. She lives with her husband, two beautiful human boys, two dogs, six fish and three equines, Ted, Bob and Happy, as well as Bailey, the next-door neighbour's pony who climbs through the fence each morning to play with the herd.

REFERENCES

Berg, S 2021, 'Why holistic view is needed to treat COVID-19 long-haul symptoms' American Medical Association, viewed 31 January 2023, <https://www.ama-assn.org/delivering-care/public-health/why-holistic-view-needed-treat-covid-19-long-haul-symptoms#:~:text=%E2%80%9CIt's%20all%20about%20access%2C%20availability,and%20access%20to%20health%20care.%E2%80%9D>

Bernard, RM, Abrami, PC, Lou, Y 2004, 'How does distance education compare with classroom instruction? A meta-analysis of the empirical literature.' *Review of Educational Research*, vol. 74, no. 3, pp. 379–439.

Burrell, A, Selman, LE 2020, 'How do funeral practices impact bereaved relatives' mental health, grief, and bereavement? A mixed methods review with implications for COVID-19' *OMEGA—Journal of Death and Dying*, vol. 85, no. 20, pp. 345–383, viewed 31 January 2023 <https://doi.org/10.1177/0030222820941296>

Chevalier, G, Sinatra, S, Oschman, J, Sokal, K, Sokal P, 2012, 'Earthing: health implications of reconnecting the human body to the Earth's surface electrons.' *Journal of environmental and public health*, vol. 2012, no. 291541, viewed 31 January 2023, <https://doi.org/10.1155/2012/291541>

Chopra, V, Flanders, SA, O'Malley, M, Malani, AN, Prescott, HC, 2021, 'Sixty-day outcomes among patients hospitalised with COVID-19', *Annals of Internal Medicine*, viewed 31 January 2023, <https://www.acpjournals.org/doi/10.7326/M20-5661>

Coelho, CM, Suttiwan, P, Arato, N, Zsido, A, 2020, 'On the nature of fear and anxiety triggered by COVID-19', *Frontiers in Psychology*, vol. 11, viewed 31 January 2023, <https://doi.org/10.3389/fpsyg.2020.581314>

Concannon, F, 2005 'What campus-based students think about the quality and benefits of e-learning', *British Journal of Educational Technology*, vol.3, no. 36, pp. 501-512.

Concannon, F, Flynn, A, Campbell, M, 2005, 'What campus-based students think about the quality and benefits of e-learning', *British Journal of Educational Technology*, vol. 36 no. 3, pp. 501–512.

Micaela, B, 2020, 'Telework in the EU before and after the COVID-19: where we were, where we head to', *European Institute for Gender Equality*, viewed 31 January 2023, <https://policycommons.net/artifacts/1950578/telework-in-the-eu-before-and-after-the-covid-19/2702347/ on 01 Feb 2023. CID: 20.500.12592/163633>

Ferguson, D, 2021, '"I feel like I'm failing": Parents' stress rises over home schooling in Covid lockdown, *The Guardian*, 24 January 2021, viewed 31 January 2023 <https://www.theguardian.com/lifeandstyle/2021/jan/23/i-feel-like-im-failing-parents-stress-rises-over-home-schooling-in-covid-lockdown>

González-Sanguine, C, Austin, B, Castellanos, MÁ, Sai, J, López-Gómez, A, Guido's, C, Muñoz, M, 2020, 'Mental health consequences during the initial stage of the 2020 Coronavirus pandemic (COVID-19) in Spain', *Brain Behavior and Immunity*, 87:172–176, viewed 31 January 2023 <https://doi.org/10.1016/j.bbi.2020.05.040>

Hemilä, H, Chalker, E, 2013, 'Vitamin C for preventing and treating the common cold', *The Cochrane database of systematic reviews*, vol. 2013,1 CD000980, viewed 31 January 2023 <https://doi.org/10.1002/14651858.CD000980.pub4>

Hemilä, H, 2017, 'Zinc lozenges and the common cold: a meta-analysis comparing zinc acetate and zinc gluconate, and the role of zinc dosage', *JRSM Open*, vol. 8 no.5, viewed 31 January 2023 <https://doi.org/10.1177/2054270417694291>

Hoge, B, 2021, 'Feeling COVID rage? Five strategies for managing pandemic anger', *UAB News*, viewed 3 March 2023, <https://www.uab.edu/news/youcanuse/item/12313-feeling-covid-rage-five-strategies-for-managing-pandemic-anger>

Hughes, A, 2021, 'New hobbies taken up in the UK during lockdown', *The Independent*, 22 March 2021, viewed 31 January 2023, <https://www.independent.co.uk/life-style/uk-lockdown-new-hobbies-pandemic-b1820506.html>

Jackson, A, 2021, 'Could your Christmas be cancelled? A therapist tells us how to soften the blow' *The Irish Times*, 16 December 2021, viewed 31 January 2023, <https://www.breakingnews.ie/lifestyle/could-your-christmas-be-cancelled-a-therapist-tells-us-how-to-soften-the-blow-1229543.html>

Kotwani, Priya et al. 2021 'A holistic care approach to combat the COVID-19 disease.' *Journal of family medicine and primary care* vol. 10,2 (2021): 844-849, viewed 31 January 2023, <https://doi.org/10.4103/jfmpc.jfmpc_1549_20>

Maxwell, E, 'Living with COVID19', *National Institute for Health and Care Research*, 15 October 2020, viewed 31 January 2023 <https://doi.org/10.3310/themedreview_41169>

McKinsey & Company, 2020, 'What's next for remote work: An analysis of 2,000 tasks, 800 jobs, and nine countries', *McKinsey.com*, viewed 31 January 2023, <https://www.mckinsey.com/featured-insights/future-of-work/whats-next-for-remote-work-an-analysis-of-2000-tasks-800-jobs-and-nine-countries>

McPeake, J, Henderson, P, MacTavish, P, Quasim, T, 2021, 'Provision of holistic care after severe COVID-19 pneumonia', *The Lancet*, viewed 31 January 2023, <https://doi.org/10.1016/S2213-2600(20)30529-4>

Mohammadi, K, 2020, 'The eyes have it: Communication and face masks', *The Guardian*, viewed 31 January 2023, <https://www.theguardian.com/lifeandstyle/2020/may/30/face-mask-eye-contact-commuication-coronavirus>

O'Connor, RC, Wetherall, K, Cleare, S, McClelland, H, Melson, AJ, Niedzwiedz, CL, O'Carroll, RE, O'Connor, DB, Platt, S, Scowcroft, E, Watson, B, Zortea, T, Ferguson, E, & Robb, KA, 2021, 'Mental health and well-being during the COVID-19 pandemic: longitudinal analyses of adults in the UK COVID-19 mental health & wellbeing study' *The British Journal of Psychiatry*, vol. 218, no. 6, pp. 326–333, viewed 31 January 2023, <https://doi.org/10.1192/bjp.2020.212>

Open Access News 2021, 'Research finds people with depression "hidden group" vulnerable to pandemic', *Open Access Government*, viewed 3 March 2023, <https://www.openaccessgovernment.org/depression-pandemic/121338/>

Organisation for Economic Co-operation and Development, 2021, 'Tackling the mental health impact of the COVID-19 crisis', *OECD.org*, viewed 31 January 2023, <https://www.oecd.org/coronavirus/policy-responses/tackling-the-mental-health-impact-of-the-covid-19-crisis-an-integrated-whole-of-society-response-0ccafa0b/>

Parker, K, Minkin, R, Bennett, J, 'Economic fallout From COVID-19 continues to hit lower-income Americans the hardest', *Pew Research Centre*, viewed 31 January 2023, <https://www.pewresearch.org/social-trends/2020/09/24/economic-fallout-from-covid-19-continues-to-hit-lower-income-americans-the-hardest/>

Pelissolo, A, Cautrès, B, Ward, J, Bibard, L, Zylberman, P, 2020 'Fear in the time of pandemic' *The Conversation (France)*, translated by Lily Parmar for *SciencesPo.fr*, viewed 31 January 2023, <https://www.sciencespo.fr/en/news/fear-in-the-time-of-pandemic>

PESI UK, 2021, 'Stress, safety and social connectedness: post-pandemic polyvagal insights', *PESI.CO.UK*, viewed 31 January 2023, <https://www.pesi.co.uk/blog/2021/july/stress-safety-and-social-connectedness>

Porges, SW, 2020, 'The COVID-19 pandemic is a paradoxical challenge to our nervous system: a polyvagal perspective', *Clinical Neuropsychiatry*, vol 17, no. 2, pp.135-138.

Ro, Christine, 2021 'How overwork is literally killing us', *BBC Worklife,* viewed 31 January 2023, <https://www.bbc.com/worklife/article/20210518-how-overwork-is-literally-killing-us>

Rodríguez-Rey, R, Garrido-Hernani, H, Collazo, S, 2020, 'Psychological impact and associated factors during the initial stage of the coronavirus (COVID-19) pandemic among the general population in Spain', *Frontiers in Psychology,* vol. 11 1540, viewed 31 January 2023, <https://doi.org/10.3389/fpsyg.2020.01540>

Rodríguez-Rey, R, Garrido-Hernansaiz, H and Bueno-Guerra, N, 2020, 'Working in the times of COVID-19: Psychological impact of the pandemic in frontline workers in Spain. *International Journal of Environmental Research and Public Health,* vol. 17, no. 21, pp.8149.

Santomauro, D, 2021, 'Global prevalence and burden of depressive and anxiety disorders in 204 countries and territories in 2020 due to the COVID-19 pandemic'. *The Lancet,* vol 398, no. 10312, pp. 1700–1712

Small, GW, Lee, J, Kaufman, A, Jalil, J, Siddarth, P, Gaddipati, H, Moody, TD, Bookheimer, SY, 2020, 'Brain health consequences of digital technology use', *Dialogues in clinical neuroscience,* vol. 22, no. 2, pp.179–187

Smith, N, Taylor, I. and Kolbas, B, 2020, 'Exploring the relationship between economic security, furlough and mental distress', *Natcen.ac.uk,* viewed 31 January 2023, <https://www.natcen.ac.uk/our-research/research/exploring-the-relationship-between-economic-security,-furlough-and-mental-distress/>

Thompson, C, Mancebo, MC, Moitra, E, 2021, 'Changes in social anxiety symptoms and loneliness after increased isolation during the COVID-19 pandemic, *Psychiatry Research,* vol. 298, no. 113834, viewed 31 January 2023, <https://doi.org/10.1016/j.psychres.2021.113834>

Thorell, LB, Skoglund, C, de la Peña, AG et al, 2021, 'Parental experiences of home-schooling during the COVID-19 pandemic: differences between seven European countries and between children with and without mental health conditions', *European Child and Adolescent Psychiatry,* viewed 31 January 2023, <https://doi.org/10.1007/s00787-020-01706-1>

UNICEF, 2021, 'COVID-19: Schools for more than 168 million children globally have been completely closed for almost a full year, says UNICEF', *Unicef.org,* viewed 31 January 2023, <https://www.unicef.org/press-releases/schools-more-168-million-children-globally-have-been-completely-closed>

United Nations, 2021a, 'Pandemic disruption to learning is an opportunity to reimagine, revitalize education', *News.un.org,* viewed 31 January 2023, <https://news.un.org/en/story/2021/01/1082792>

REFERENCES

United Nations, 2021b, 'Over 168 million children miss nearly a year of schooling', News.un.org, viewed 31 January 2023, <https://news.un.org/en/story/2021/03/1086232#:~:text=Over%20168%20million%20children%20miss%20nearly%20a%20year%20of%20schooling%2C%20UNICEF%20says,-UNICEF%2FChris%20Farber&text=UNICEF's%20'Pandemic%20Classroom'%20at%20the,have%20been%20almost%20entirely%20closed>

Wagner, 2016, 'Polyvagal theory in practice', *Counseling Today*, viewed 31 January 2023, <https://ct.counseling.org/2016/06/polyvagal-theory-practice/>

Wagner, B, Knaevelsrud, C, Maercker, A, 2006, 'Internet-based cognitive-behavioural therapy for complicated grief: A randomized controlled trial', *Death Studies*, vol. 30, no. 5, pp. 429–453

Watts, R, 2021, 'A second layer of loss': Pandemic has changed how we grieve for our loved ones', *HealthyDebate.ca*, viewed 31 January 2023, <https://healthydebate.ca/2021/08/topic/pandemic-death-rituals-funerals/>

West, CP, Derby, LN, Shanafelt, TD, 2018, 'Physician burnout: Contributors, consequences, and solutions' *Journal of Internal Medicine*; vol. 283, no. 6, pp. 516–529, viewed 31 January 2023, <https://doi.org/10.1111/joim.12752>

The World Bank, 2020, 'Pandemic threatens to push 72 million more children into learning poverty', *Worldbank.org*, viewed 31 January 2023, <https://www.worldbank.org/en/news/press-release/2020/12/02/pandemic-threatens-to-push-72-million-more-children-into-learning-poverty-world-bank-outlines-new-vision-to-ensure-that-every-child-learns-everywhere#:~:text=WASHINGTON%2C%20December%202%2C%202020%20%E2%80%93,World%20Bank%20reports%20released%20today>

Have you thought about incorporating horses into your practice? In addition to loving horses there are many factors to consider if you want to include them in your work. Naomi Rossthorn, a registered psychologist, has the hoofprints – theory and practicalities – for incorporating horses into your psychology or therapy practice, and partnering with therapy horses for human wellness.

In 2010, Naomi developed an adjunct trauma sensitive Experiential Horse Therapy Program for those affected by the 2009 Black Saturday bushfires in Victoria, Australia. The program was delivered to children, adolescents, and adults.

Since then, she has developed and co-facilitated Equine-Assisted therapy and Psychology programs for children and adolescents exposed to complex family environments, as well as trauma-sensitive programs for people affected by natural disasters, including bushfire affected communities and more recently, the COVID-19 pandemic. A wealth of experience is delivered here in *Hoofprints*.

Hoofprints brings Naomi's life experiences, training, and professional skill to the fore, wrapped up in her passion for safe and effective equine-assisted therapy. I know you'll love this book!
Dr Tess Crawley, Psychologist & Business Coach

I highly recommend Hoofprints to any health professional who is interested to learn more about Equine-Assisted Psychology and its application within the mental health, allied health, and general health field.
Gerda Muller, Clinical Psychologist, author & mentor

REFERENCES

All Horses Become the Stars is a children's book about grief and loss. A tale told of a beloved horse called Trigger who becomes a star and the journey of how his herd cope with their loss. This book is written with children in mind and offers a way to discuss grief and healing after losing someone we love.

Trigger was a big, strong horse that worries a lot. He worries about tigers eating him and the wind in the trees. Luckily, Trigger has Happy to talk to.

Trigger learns that it's normal to feel like he does and that there are ways to help himself feel better.

Feeling sad can happen to us sometimes. There are many things that we can do to make ourselves happier, just like Happy the pony did. What makes YOU happy?

www.ingramcontent.com/pod-product-compliance
Lightning Source LLC
Chambersburg PA
CBHW041319110526
44591CB00021B/2840